Bernadette
Nguyenai
Jim
Kathleen.
Bevan
Deirdre
Leisa
Patrick
colour

INVISIBLE LIVES

Stories of Adults with Learning Disabilities

Michael Cole

DESTiNED

GUILDHALL PRESS

First published in November 2009

DESTiNED
Empowering People with
Learning Disabilities
15 Princes Street
Derry
BT48 7EY
T: 00 44 28 7136 2424
W: www.destined.ie

GUILDHALL PRESS
Ráth Mór Business Park
Creggan, Derry
BT48 0LZ
T: 00 44 28 7136 4413
E: info@ghpress.com
W: www.ghpress.com

Disclaimer
The views expressed in the stories that follow are those of the
interviewees and nobody else's. This is the first time most of them have
spoken publicly. Any comments about third parties or agencies are
made, fairly, in the understanding that these parties or agencies have
told their stories publicly before.

The
Community Foundation
for Northern Ireland

Invisible Lives was supported
by the Turkington Fund which is
administered by The Community
Foundation for Northern Ireland.

PRODUCTION TEAM

Reporters
Michael Cole
Patrick Lavery
Darryl McDonough
Róisín O'Hara
Jim O'Reilly

Design
Cover: Jim Collins, Denise Meenan and the Destined members
Inside: Guildhall Press

Photography
Eugene Harron and Colm Canavan

Production Manager
Colm Canavan

Copy Editors
Donncha Mac Niallais
Kenny Martin
Michael Dobbins
Caroline O'Hara

Editor
Garbhan Downey

Publisher
Dermot O'Hara

ACKNOWLEDGEMENTS

Many thanks to all those who contributed: to the Destined leaders Terry McDevitt, Martina Coyle and Catherine; to Michael Dobbins, Nuala Begley and Áine Downey for their most valuable advice; to all at Guildhall Press for their support and professional expertise; to our production team; to Paul Diamond, Diamond Corrugated Casings, for his most generous support; and to our very benevolent sponsors, The Community Foundation for Northern Ireland, without whom this project would have remained just another good idea.

*To the volunteers who work
with Destined*

CONTENTS

PREFACE

Several years ago, Mary Nelis, a local elected member of the Northern Ireland Assembly, invited the Destined group to visit Stormont Buildings in Belfast. It was a fantastic day, as all the politicians were there that day as part of the

Dermot O'Hara

ongoing negotiations regarding the peace process. The Destined members had their photographs taken with Gerry Adams, Martin McGuinness, Mark Durkan, Ian Paisley and David Trimble to mention but a few.

Destined had also arranged to meet with another learning disability group based in East Belfast while on the visit, and there was a much quieter encounter happening in this big building on the hill. Dympna Markey had just met a friend whom she had not seen since the early 1970s when they were both living in Muckamore Abbey in Antrim. Later, when recounting the surprise meeting with me, I realised the depth of history Dympna possessed about the institutions and the hidden experiences of people with learning disabilities. I decided that day that there was a need to record the stories of people like Dympna.

A short while ago on a Monday evening one of the Destined members came into the office for a chat while waiting for the Irish class to begin. I asked him how the weekend went, and he said that they were at a nightclub in Letterkenny. I asked him why they go there rather than to clubs in Derry, and he said that it stays open until four in the morning. Up until three years before, this person spent most of his time in his bedroom, with no friends and no social activities. He was part of that large group of people with learning disabilities who are isolated from, and invisible to, the community.

Change is coming, and change is happening, for people with learning disabilities. The days of people living in isolation at home are ending, and this book is about people saying, 'Here I am and this is my story.' It is a statement of intent that is telling society that we have arrived and we are part of this community – all aspects of it. This book is a celebration of life, both the hardships and the good times; it is a celebration of survival.

It is a statement of maturity from people who know where they have come from and where they are going and who are saying to this community you have been privileged with our stories, read them well for the future.

Dermot O'Hara
Project Manager
Destined

INTRODUCTION

Making the invisible visible

Garbhan Downey

Many of us like to think we could write a book about our lives, but very few of us actually see it through. We worry that our triumphs, disasters, loves and losses mightn't, somehow, be interesting enough to other people. We assure ourselves our lives aren't that relevant. So, for the most part, the field is left to the important and self-important among us.

I spent many years as a journalist interviewing people who had stories to tell; athletes, politicians, entertainers, business leaders, academics, clerics and paramilitaries. And, while their lives were undoubtedly interesting, and in some cases even heroic, I was always conscious that they weren't really any more interesting, or heroic, than most of the other ordinary civilians I knew. Pat McArt, then editor of the *Derry Journal*, agreed, and commissioned me to write a weekly series entitled 'Everyday Folk', in which we would profile somebody not normally seen on the media radar. And it worked like a charm. Unsung lives, I quickly discovered, were all the more intriguing than public ones – precisely because they had never been explored. So when I got the opportunity to help with Destined's new book, charting never-before-told life histories, I leapt at it.

It was Dermot O'Hara, I must stress, and not me, who coined the term 'Invisible Lives' as the most appropriate title for this project. People with learning disabilities, he reasoned, spend large parts of their lives completely unseen by society. Dermot's daughter Róisín, a founding director of Destined, summed it up very succinctly, in her interview, when she said: "People would ask my mum and dad, 'How's Róisín doing?' And I would be sitting there, thinking, 'Why don't you talk to me?' I felt invisible."

I was little better. As a reporter, I would have spoken occasionally to teachers, social workers and carers about the needs of people with learning disabilities, but until I started working on this project, I'd never sought the opinions of the people most directly affected themselves. Even yet, in recent meetings with Destined members, I have found myself politely upbraided for failing to listen fully and properly. As Michael Dobbins, principal of Foyle View School, pointed out, the real learning difficulty lies with society – or in this case with me. And it's not so much that the lives recounted here were always invisible, but rather that the wider public chose to be blind to them.

In the summer of 2009, the Destined group took the decision to compile, in the form of a book, their experiences as adults who had grown up, and live every day, with learning disabilities.

The group felt it was also important to record the experiences of their parents, friends and guardians – those described by Bernie Gallagher as "quiet heroes and heroines, who have made great contributions to this earth, but never get, or seek, any credit".

To this end, I was asked to facilitate a series of interviews, the format of which was decided by Destined members, who then conducted the dialogues themselves. The interviews were then transcribed by Destined members, and edited, after which the group reviewed and amended the work before sanctioning the final draft.

The cover of the book was also designed by the Destined group, in conjunction with Jim Collins of the Bluebell Arts Project. And any and all publishing expenses were paid out by the Destined committee, who sourced the funding for the project and organised the book launch as well. Importantly, the group also set a series of deadlines, to ensure a pre-Christmas publication, and didn't miss a single one of them. My involvement was solely that of editor.

The standard of interviewing, as I witnessed time and again, was of the highest journalistic quality. The reporters agreed a comprehensive set of questions (included as an appendix) – and then showed flair in following up loose ends and pursuing new lines of enquiry.

But if the questioning was professional, the responses were illuminating. This book provides first-hand insights on everything from institutional abuse to parental sacrifice; from bullying and intolerance to friendship and joy. Every single story here has something different to tell you. Something unique to teach you.

Moreover, the stories here are not in any way negative in tone. Quite the reverse. They are uplifting, positive and almost universally uncomplaining. There is little grievance, but boundless gratitude; little blame, but frequent tribute. The book is a celebration, not a court of inquiry.

There are many things I hope you take away from this book. You might find yourself asking why some people with learning disabilities are expected to work for nothing while the people standing beside them, doing the same job, are paid a full salary. You might wonder why, of all the people with learning difficulties interviewed here, only one is in a long-term relationship. Or you might find yourself perplexed at a system which tells a person it's in their own best interests to spend half their life in an institution; and this person then goes on and adapts immediately to the "freedom" of semi-independent living as soon as they are offered the chance.

You will be comforted, no doubt, by the fact that education and health provision for people with learning difficulties has improved greatly during the lifetimes of those interviewed. The unfolding human rights agenda has also made a massive difference. Indeed, you can track the societal changes, and what these changes have meant, through the stories here. But it is also essential to remember that there is still a long way to go, as carer Paula McNamara explained: "Many people with disabilities can't get a job despite their skills. The services aren't joined up and are underfunded. Fantastic case workers are overstretched, and because of this, young people are left stuck at home."

Destined have shown that they are not prepared to accept the "stay at home" option any longer. They pursue a goal of full inclusion and empowerment, seven days a week, through a never-ending schedule of activities and a thriving drop-in centre. They campaign for the right to paid employment and access to full citizenship. And they do all this in a spirit of fun and kinship that leaves other organisations running to catch up.

In short, the Destined members have made the invisible visible, and for this, we must thank them. Most importantly of all, however, we must see them now and listen to their stories.

Garbhan Downey, October 2009

13

CHAPTER 1

The Invisible Lives of Adults with Learning Disabilities

The stories that follow were derived from interviews conducted at Destined's offices in Princes Street, during September 2009. All those who took part did so willingly, and they subsequently approved the final text of their stories prior to publication.

The terminology used here varies slightly – with some interviewees using the term "learning difficulty", others using "learning disability" and others again using both. In most cases, the term used by the reporters was "learning difficulty".

The stories here are of varying lengths, some are short and sweet, others longer and reflective. There was no maximum or minimum word limit; the interviewee dictated the pace.

What is very apparent through these stories is how society's response to people with learning difficulties has changed, mostly for the better, over the past 60 years. So, to give the reader a sense of that, we decided to present the stories in chronological order, with the eldest interviewees first.

I NEVER SAW THE OUTSIDE WORLD

'The nuns used to wear belts on their waists and hit the children with them... I used to tell people outside. No one took any heed of us.'
Bernadette Bradley

Bernadette Bradley, who's now 64, was schooled in Dublin before moving to Derry, where she worked for more than 30 years in a laundry and in various factories. Following a serious illness, she became a long-term resident of Stradreagh Hospital, which also served as an institution for people with learning difficulties, after which she transferred to sheltered accommodation at Ardavon House.

"I was born in the middle of Ulster on June 27, 1945, and baptised. Then my mother put me into Fahan [orphanage] with the nuns, and I stayed there till I was a year old. My mother was single – she was Bridget Bradley. I don't know my father's name.

"I went to Nazareth House in Bishop Street when I was three, then I went to Dublin at five years of age. The reason I went there was because I was slower at picking up than the rest of the children. I coped better in Dublin. I learned a lot, and I was on a history book when I left school. I got a lot of help in Dublin and liked the school. It was called the Sisters of Charity. The nuns were kind to me."

Bernadette had lots of friends at her Dublin school – and even after she moved back home, she would swap letters with them.

"I was very, very close to them. I had three particular friends, and we used to go out in the fields, climbing up the trees for apples or gathering potatoes. I used to throw the potatoes at the horses, and they would run around the field. I was never caught but, and I enjoyed it.

"We used to play mammies and daddies down the field and make rag dolls for bed. We used to make our own fun because we were never loved, you know. I never knew my mother at all."

At the age of 15, Bernadette left school to return to Nazareth House in Derry, to work in the priest's parlour. It was shortly after this that her health began to decline.

"I worked in the parlour first, then I went into the sewing room to learn how to machine. Then after that I went to the kitchen. I didn't eat for a while and my health got bad, and I went into a clinic. It was the nuns that made me go because I was too far down. I was happy to do that because I wanted to get well.

"When I went to Stradreagh Hospital, I learned I had a disability. In Stradreagh we were treated the same, but we never knew what the outside world was like because we were inside all the time. When I went out, I wanted to go back again because I wasn't used to the outside world."

Bernadette was sent to work in the Good Shepherd laundry in the Waterside, a facility run by nuns. She found the labour hard. And she says the treatment of the workers there sometimes verged on abuse.

"I had to work hard on the presser in the laundry. We

didn't get paid, but we got our keep, nothing more. We didn't get money at all. They just bought us things like soaps, toothpaste, brushes and combs. But we never got money.

"Some of the nuns were hard. Some of them used to hit the children, though there were also some good ones. No one took any heed of us. They didn't listen to us when we did tell.

"I used to tell people outside. They say it's all behind us now. I don't know; it's all coming out now. The nuns used to wear belts on their waists and hit the children with them. I wasn't hit because I was a bit older."

Bernadette went on to get work in the shirt factories, and later at the Essex plant in Creggan, which made car parts.

"When I was working, I got paid a full wage. I was happy with that, and I was well treated. I think I was the only one from Stradreagh who worked in the factory at that time. I used to go out at quarter past seven in the bus, and sometimes I slept in. I would go out the door with a boiled egg and toast to the bus with me. The factories started very early.

"Most of them were very good to me at the factory. I was one of the number ones; I did the front of the shirts and hem pockets.

"Essex was mad. We used to bang the machines and all when the holidays were coming up; we were all excited. When someone was getting married, we used to pull them in a go-cart right around the yard, down and up, down and up. We didn't take the clothes off them like they do to fellas. I don't think the women are involved in that."

There was one incident when Bernadette was picked on by one of her co-workers because of her disability. But the factory acted promptly and the offender, a supervisor, was moved. Bernadette made a lot of good friends in the factories and is still in contact with Teresa, who would always keep a particular eye out for her.

"She is married now with two children, but she always keeps in touch with me. She's very good to me. She would come in to visit me and look after me."

In 1978, Bernadette moved out of Stradreagh and into Ardavon House, which she really likes.

"The carers are good. I get on with them all. I have had no problems."

At one stage, she did have a serious boyfriend, but she is now very content with the single life.

"I am happy with the way my life went. I have no husband; I used to go with boys, but it didn't work out. I went with a fella from Limavady and got engaged to him in Faller's Jewellers. But I gave him back the ring. He was a bit older than me. He got furniture but he didn't get a house. I said to him, 'What use is furniture if you haven't got a house?'"

In her spare time, Bernadette makes her own cards, arranges flowers and studies art. She also enjoys reading history and watching the soaps.

Bernadette is convinced that the support for people with learning disabilities has improved greatly over her lifetime. And she is a particular advocate of Destined.

"I never went out until I went to Destined. It's really brilliant. I really enjoy it, and Dermot is a great manager. I love it because it takes me out, and you meet people that you never met.

"When I was in Stradreagh, I never saw the outside world. I was indoors all the time. I was hidden away; then

18

when I did go out I wasn't used to it. I wanted to go back in again.

"Now, we go a lot of places with Destined – up to the Old Library Trust to learn First Aid and to the gym. I was in the gym today and it was very, very good. There is something different all the time. It's really great."

I NEVER LET IT HOLD ME BACK

'My mother didn't know there was anything different about me till I left school.'
Colm Cusack

Colm Cusack, who is best known as the smiling face welcoming all and sundry to Destined's offices, worked in factories for most of his life, before becoming house manager at Princes Street.

Colm, who's now 64, grew up in Creggan where he still lives with his brother and sister-in-law.

"We've lived in Melmore Gardens since I was about four. We were a happy family growing up. We used to play football – I wasn't good but I enjoyed playing. It passed the time. We also played Cowboys and Indians. In my family there are three boys and three girls, and they would all look out for me.

"I was about fifteen years old when I learned I had a learning disability. I'd been to St Eugene's [primary school], where I got on well. Mr Duffy was the principal. And Danny McLaughlin, who was a teacher there, lived across the street from me. He was a good neighbour. I was never bullied at school.

"My mother didn't know there was anything different about me till I left school. The doctors diagnosed me. It was a bit of a shock, but I didn't let it hold me back."

Shortly after leaving school, Colm was involved in a bad accident, when he was exploring the abandoned Foyle Hill hospital, close to his Creggan home.

"I was up there messing around when part of the wall from in-between the windows fell on my foot. It was very serious; I was in Altnagelvin Hospital for three weeks, and they sent me to a hospital in Belfast for a skin graft. Even now, part of my heel isn't flat and I wear different shoes. I won't be doing that again! The people in the hospital were good to me. There was a young woman, a patient of about fifteen or sixteen, who would come in to talk to me and make sure I was all right."

After he recovered, Colm enrolled in the workshops for people with learning disabilities, based on the Northland Road.

"I did a lot of things there, like making wire hangers for coats in the dry cleaners and stapling shirt collars and straps. No one really picked on me. They were good to me, and I could look after myself."

After a brief placement with Diamond Corrugated Casings in Pennyburn, Colm then got a full-time job in the United Technologies factory in Creggan.

"I worked on the machines cutting wire harnesses for the Ford Motor Company. I was there for nineteen-and-a-half years. It closed in 1997. I enjoyed it there. It was good craic. Sometimes they would slag you off, and I would give it back. I wasn't treated differently. I was treated just as one of the workers. I was happy with that.

"We would sometimes get up to mischief. Like when someone was going to get married, we would cover them in eggs and flour – nothing too bad. The supervisors were good to me, like when I was bad with asthma, they let me off for six weeks. That gave me time to recover."

Outside work, Colm led a very quiet life. He didn't socialise with his co-workers, nor did he visit pubs.

"I didn't have a girlfriend, but a girl asked me out once. I refused because it involved a third party. I like a girl to ask me directly. But she asked someone else to ask me."

Even today, Colm rarely goes out at night. He doesn't like the dark and worries that the town has become a bit dangerous. "Someone might come over and give you a thump. I have only been to bars once or twice. I am happy to stay out of them."

After United Technologies closed, Colm tended to stay at home, where he would indulge his passion for rug-making. He still sends away for kits and makes rugs himself. He also enjoys word puzzles and watching TV, with *CSI Miami* top of his current list of favourite shows.

Six years ago, however, he became involved with Destined and soon discovered his new vocation.

"I would be known as the funny guy in Destined. They would be lost without me. I am also the house manager. I go and buy the stuff that is needed and keep the place clean. Sometimes I would tell other people to do stuff.

"Part of my job is to open up the centre and welcome people. And if any women come in, I give them a hug and a kiss!

"I like my job in Destined. I spend a lot of time at the centre. I sometimes slag off the staff, and they slag me back but nothing too serious. They are very good and supportive."

As a younger man, Colm had ambitions to become a security man but never got to do it.

"I haven't any qualifications. But I sometimes do courses at Destined, like computers. In fact, I am working my way through three courses at the minute – chips, peas and gravy!"

PEOPLE DON'T GET PUT DOWN ANY MORE

'I was the eejit of the class.
I was punished for things
I didn't do.'
Hugh Hegarty

Hugh Hegarty, who is 64, lives in sheltered accommodation in the Waterside. A former factory worker, he is a lifelong Derry City fan.

Hugh had a happy childhood and was looked after well by his family. "I grew up on the Lone Moor Road and lived there for fifty years. I have two brothers and two sisters. I get on well with them. I used to play football but not with my brothers and sisters. My brother played tennis.

"I have never spent any time in foster care or been in an institution for people with learning disabilities."

Hugh's learning disability was discovered at school. And at times he was picked on because of it.

"I was kept back a year when I was transferring from the wee school to the big school. The teachers didn't bother much with me. I was treated differently because of my learning disability. I was the eejit of the class. I don't remember any of the teachers being particularly good to me. At times, I was punished for things I didn't do."

Hugh left school without qualifications, although one teacher did spend extra time with him to ensure he had grounding in English and Maths.

He got a job in a factory in Maydown as a packer, where he got on very well with the people he worked with.

Now retired, Hugh enjoys reading, watching TV and socialising with his friends from Destined. He loves football and used to attend Derry matches with the Creggan Supporters' Club [since disbanded] and his brother. He is happy to be single.

Hugh believes that support for people with learning disabilities has improved significantly over his lifetime.

"It's far better. People don't get put down any more."

I WAS AN EASY TARGET

'I didn't want to be there. I didn't know I was going there. They didn't tell me. They said I was going somewhere nice.'
Dympna Markey

Dympna Markey, who was born in 1950, never knew her family. She spent much of her life in institutions, first in Nazareth House when she was a baby, then she moved to Muckamore Abbey in Antrim and on to Stradreagh Hospital, before finally settling in sheltered accommodation at Ardavon House on Derry's Northland Road. She has worked on placements in the catering industry, most recently at Cafe Rosa on Bishop Street and Bloom's Cafe in the Verbal Arts Centre.

"When I was a child I didn't like school, because of some people taunting me. I think they were jealous of me. I had difficulty with speech when I was young. I talk too quickly. I went and got help in Antrim, and learned how to speak slowly. I found out I had a learning disability at that time.

"I can't really read. And I get annoyed sometimes when there are words I can't say. And I'm not very good with numbers. But I am getting help in Destined. It's my own fault because I was carrying on in school."

Dympna's guardians were the concert impresario Don O'Doherty and his wife Mary McLaughlin, and they were very good to her. Unfortunately, Dympna's memories of Muckamore Abbey, where many children with learning difficulties were institutionalised in the 1950s and 1960s, are less pleasant.

"Mary and Don wanted to take me out for weekends but the people there said no. So they said they would take me overnight, and the staff wouldn't allow it. I used to wonder if some of them had a spite against me.

"Another time, Mary and Don were supposed to come up and see me in Antrim, but something happened and they couldn't come. It upset me. I was waiting, and they never came. It wasn't their fault, but I was in a very bad way about it. It's all in the past though. I got over it."

Dympna was frequently in bother at Muckamore but felt she was also an easy target for people to blame when things went wrong.

"I didn't like school. I was always in trouble and faced to a wall. That's why I went to Antrim. Once, someone broke a window by throwing stones at it, and I got blamed for it. I didn't do it though. I was sometimes bullied because of my disability, not really bad. I didn't like it. It happened some of my other friends as well.

"I wasn't lonely in Antrim. I had some friends; Robert, Mary and Nina. We enjoyed singing and playing bowls. Lesley was very good to me too. My learning disability never worried me. Antrim was all right after I met Nina. We had parties. Nina would stand up for me if I got my hair pulled."

The staff at Muckamore would occasionally allow the girls out of their quarters. And Dympna had a number of friendships with local boys.

"I used to go with a fella in Antrim. He wasn't nice – in fact he was horrible, drank like a fish. We nearly got engaged but I turned him down. God help the poor girl he married. Mary and Don heard about it and weren't happy with it. I was caught and got caned by one of the staff.

"There were some people I met who were very kind to me, though. Sister Aidan, who was from Belfast, was very good to me."

After Muckamore, Dympna was transferred into full-time care at Stradreagh Hospital, where she lived for "many" years. She doesn't feel she was given any choice about the move at all.

"I didn't want to be there. I didn't know I was going there. They didn't tell me. They said I was going somewhere nice. Some of people there were not very nice and got me into trouble."

Dympna, however, was always quick to stand up for herself. And she got into trouble for slapping a fellow resident because he was picking on her.

"I didn't mean to do it and I shouldn't have done it. I learned my lesson. I should have walked away."

Dympna worked for a while in Stradreagh Hospital. Then, through her friend Jim Doherty, "a very good person", she got a job in the canteen at Altnagelvin.

"In Stradreagh, I worked in the patient canteen on Saturday and Sunday, and the staff canteen during the week. Then I went to work with Jim. I liked working with Jim, but I left once Jim left. After that, I was working in another cafe, but I left because I didn't get on with a couple of the younger ones.

"I would like to work in a canteen or a hotel. A restaurant would be a good place to make friends."

Dympna was glad to move out of Stradreagh to Ardavon House, which gives her a lot more independence. She is a little worried about retiring from her job next year as she will miss the company. But she intends to stay in touch with all her work colleagues.

She has a wide range of hobbies, from singing to listening to music – Elvis is a particular favourite – to bowling, to table-tennis. She also loves watching the soaps, films and documentaries about animals.

Dympna is comforted by the fact that, when she does retire, Destined will help keep her schedule full.

"I have lots of friends now in Ardavon and in Destined. I like Destined because you get to go out. Dermot [O'Hara] is a really good person and a good laugh. Support for people with learning disabilities is great now – I'm as happy as Larry.

"I like Róisín [Róisín O'Hara, Destined director]. She was a good laugh on the holidays. I missed Róisín last year. We all went to Blackpool. Bernadette and I went to the wrong hotel but they found us. I liked Blackpool. Frank Carson lives there now. He's an eejit. He knew me as a youngster – I like him."

I WAS AN OLYMPIC GOLD MEDAL WINNER

'I've been in Macbeth, The Tractor, The Pink Elephants and the next one will be Doctor Watt's Stewbox. I don't mind learning the lines; it's not too bad.'
George Harkin

George Harkin, who was born in 1960, had a happy childhood, growing up with his six brothers and three sisters on Marlborough Road. After a stint at Pennyburn PS, he went to Rosemount Boys and then to St Joseph's Secondary School, where, he says, his learning disability was never an issue with his teachers.

"At times I found school hard," he recalls. "I can read and write well enough, but I found dividing and some maths difficult.

"A couple of times I might have been punished unfairly – strapped because I didn't know answers. But I got on very well with the boys in the class, never felt left out – always had plenty of company."

There was, however, the odd troublemaker.

"There were a couple of boys at St Joe's who took the hand out of me and would pick on me. Most of the time I ignored them. But I had to report some.

"Once I got into a scrap about it. Only once. The teacher

said to me afterwards he couldn't believe I'd done it – stepping out of line like that."

After leaving school, George went to the adult training centre on Northland Road, making picture frames, mop-heads, and labels for the DuPont factory.

He then moved to the centre at Maybrook, where he discovered his talent for indoor bowling.

"A lady called Teresa O'Kane began training us at the Bowling Alley and entering us into competitions. We won those and eventually got to the Olympics in Dublin, where I won two gold medals! I was very proud of myself. The last guy I had to beat, on the day before we came home, had a score of 147. But I got 174.

"We came home and had celebrations back at the centre, and got our photos taken for the paper."

After leaving Maybrook, George applied his woodwork skills in the picture-framing department at Stradreagh, where, in his spare time, he also made transport boxes for fish-merchants.

He later joined the PHAB (Physically Handicapped Able Bodied) group on Pump Street, working as a charity collector. PHAB also had their own Derry City Supporters Club, which he took part in. And today, almost 20 years on, he still goes to matches at the Brandywell with Terry McDevitt, the Destined leader, and several of his friends from the Destined group.

For the last five years, George has worked with the Lilliput Theatre Company, the North's only professional company for adults with learning disabilities, based at Derry's Playhouse.

The troupe has toured successfully across Ireland,

producing everything from Macbeth to comedy sketches.

"It's good craic. Gordon Smith and Maureen Clark who run the group are great people. I like it very much. At the minute we're doing sketches for Owen Barr. And we've done lots of plays. I've been in Macbeth, The Tractor, The Pink Elephants and the next one will be Doctor Watt's Stewbox. I don't mind learning the lines; it's not too bad."

George lived with his parents until October 2005, when he made the move to semi-independent living at the Methodist Mission on Crawford Square.

"It was my first time living on my own. And I've been getting on very well. Sean Boyle [the manager] has been very good to me. I'm able to look after myself pretty well – I can cook and manage my own money and medication. My brother, who's my carer, can't always be there to help me out. My sisters are there most of the time. And I still visit my parents regularly – two or three times a week."

The medication is necessary to control George's epilepsy, which was formerly quite severe and caused his hospitalisation. But his latest regimen has proved very successful, and he hasn't had an attack "in a long time". "I pray I never have another," he says.

Because of his condition, George will never be allowed to drive. Though this doesn't particularly concern him. Much more worrying was the mini-stroke he suffered two years ago, at the age of 46, which left him with a weakness in his right leg.

Besides his work with Lilliput, George helps out in the Methodist Mission part-time, cleaning the floors and setting the tables. "I enjoy it very much."

Outside work, George likes to meet up with his friends at the Destined Centre or head out on day-trips with the group.

"Destined is a great place to relax during the day – if you want to have a chat, or muck in helping cooking or making the tea.

"I've done a few classes here – the Irish course, and couple of others I can't remember.

"And I like the rambling, or going to the pictures or the gym. The staff are all excellent, and I get on very well with Dermot. He's a very nice man, down-to-earth."

George believes conditions for people with learning disabilities have improved since he was young.

"I think it's better now. There's more support now. Groups like Destined here on Princes Street are very important. I like Destined very much, and I hope more places like Destined open up for everyone. I have come a long way since I joined the Destined Club, and I think things have improved over the years."

I'M FAR FROM STUPID

'I was involved in an accident in Washington DC in 1966. It damaged the talking part of the brain. I stutter and I have to repeat things to people. If this accident hadn't happened, I wouldn't have the problems I have now.'
Michael McEvoy

Michael McEvoy, who wrote his own contribution, works part time as a librarian and lives with his parents. He is happily single.

I was born on May 26, 1963 in Norfolk, Virginia. It is on the eastern seaboard of the United States. We moved to New Orleans, Louisiana back in 1964. Then we moved to Washington DC, when I was three years old. We moved to Londonderry in the United Kingdom in July 1967; the reason for coming over here – my dad was in the United States Navy. We have been here ever since. I am still an American after 42 years.

I am the oldest of five children, and family life was happy and normal. I played football and went swimming.

I was involved in an accident in Washington DC in 1966. It damaged the talking part of the brain. I have got a speech defect. I stutter and I have to repeat things to people. Also, I have got a limp in the right leg. If this accident hadn't happened, I wouldn't have the problems I have now. I have still got a problem in accepting this. I am a little bit angry over this accident at times. Some doctors ran me through a battery of tests in 1971 and 1983. These doctors could find nothing wrong with me.

I attended Belmont School from April 6, 1971 to June 29, 1979. I had no problems at this school in connection with the speech defect. In general, my teachers were very helpful and good to me. But there were a few teachers who were downright cheeky. The boys and the girls were good to me.

[Belmont House School caters for a wide range of special needs including moderate learning difficulties, language disorders, and emotional and behaviour difficulties.]

When I was five years old, back in 1968, my mother took me to a circus. The clown went to other children but would not come near me. People called me "sp-----c" and mocked me and were putting me down. It was not very nice for me at all. I was called a "stupid b-----d" and "empty-head". Me being stupid. Far from it. I have got a razor-sharp mind. I am very good at history and military history. I have been driving a car for the last eight years. I passed the driving test, first time, on December 13, 2001. It doesn't bother me any more when people call me names.

I went to the Glenbrook Day Centre from September 1980 to June 26, 1981 and Melrose Day Centre from August 20, 1985 to June 10, 1994. I have been coming to Destined, on and off, since September 2003. At the Melrose centre and Destined, I had great times. I talked to people, watched the TV, went to bowls and had fun. I didn't like Glenbrook – people in their sixties and seventies. I was only 17 years old back then.

Over the past nine years, I have studied computing in Tullyally and the Strand Tech [North West Regional College]. And I am doing a cooking course up in Strabane Tech [also NWRC]. This course started on September 10, 2008 – another two more years to go.

I worked in Brooke Park Library from September 1979 to August 1980. 'Young Help' got me this job; they were based in Pump Street in the town.

I started working with Sow & Grow on April 13, 1992. I have been there for 17 years. The staff are very good to me. I weed, and I do the dinner list. But I find it monotonous. I get on well with some of the workers.

I had three jobs from August 1999 to December 2000, but they went pear-shaped. New Horizons got me these jobs. They are based up in Strabane and find jobs for people with learning problems.

New Horizons got me a job at the library in Finn House, Stradreagh. I started this job on April 24, 2001, Tuesdays and Thursdays from 1.00pm to 4.00pm. Finn House moved to Lakeview in September 2005, and I am at the library just on Thursdays now.

If I pass the cooking course I am taking, I would like to work in a restaurant and meet people.

I spend my spare time reading books about military history, from October 1066 up to the Gulf War II in March 2003. I go to bowls – and am very good at this. I also go on the computer and watch TV. At weekends, my friends and I like to go out for runs in the car. I drive the car.

[See also: Mary Joe McEvoy on page 75]

DESTINED HAS MADE A BIG DIFFERENCE

'Before Destined it was hard to go out and do things. I stayed in the house, sitting doing nothing.'
Deirdre McGuinness

Deirdre McGuinness, who's 44, works with the Lilliput Theatre Company at the Playhouse. She grew up in Creggan, and in 1985 she moved to Beechwood Avenue with her parents, where she still lives.

"We were a happy family. My mother and father got married when they were very young. They got married in St. Mary's Chapel [Creggan] at nine in the morning then went to Buncrana for their honeymoon. My father used to live on Lecky Road with his brothers and sisters. There were five of them in the one bed. In them times they had no money."

Deirdre, who has three brothers and five sisters, was born with displaced hips and had to wear specially-made shoes as a child. She went to Belmont House Special School, when it still took in boarders, though she was there as a day-pupil. (The school stopped taking boarders in 1986.)

"I coped grand at school, but some of the things they were teaching us were kind of hard. Sometimes the teachers would be telling you to do stuff while you were trying to concentrate on another question. Some questions were hard, and some were okay.

"I liked Mrs Logan. I got on well with her. She was a good teacher. I don't think I was ever punished because of my learning difficulties. I took part in all the concerts in the school. I learned to read and write and do numbers."

The Belmont pupils, Deirdre recalls, would occasionally get up to high jinks.

"I remember it being Patrick's birthday, and they put his head under the water tap. He ended up being sick. I think one of the teachers must have got on to whoever did it. I was there, but I wasn't involved. I wouldn't do things like that. I was well-behaved at school. I never got in trouble."

After leaving school at 16, Deirdre stayed at home for a few months, before getting a place at the adult training centre on Northland Road.

"I was there for a few years. Us girls did hospital work upstairs, like packing gauze into bags and sending it to Altnagelvin. And the boys were downstairs doing picture framing. I liked it there; it was somewhere to go every day, instead of staying at home. The girls were good fun as well.

"The building was getting old, so they got a new one on the Racecourse Road called the Maybrook Adult Training Centre and we moved. [George Harkin also transferred at this time.] I was in there for a very long time. I worked in the office answering phones and things like that. I liked it there. I was a receptionist and did stuff for the secretary as well."

After Maybrook, Deirdre had a brief spell at the workshop at Stradreagh, before embarking on a new career in drama with the Lilliput Company. The troupe was established by former Stradreagh staff and is now the resident company at the Derry Playhouse.

"Gordon Smith, who was taking the group up at the Playhouse, asked me to join, and I have been there ever since. I am up there all the time. On a Monday I go to the Tech for pottery classes, and on Thursday, we study education and computers. I like the Playhouse now it's done up. The new building is lovely. The old one was falling to the ground – it was very old.

"We have just finished a production called 'Hope in the Derry Workshop'. It was about all the people who lived there and were separated from their families. I acted in it, and Gordon Smith directed with another member of staff. I enjoy working in the Playhouse because we get the opportunity to do performances at community centres. We would go out in our minibus."

Deirdre doesn't believe her learning disability has had an adverse effect on her life – despite the very occasional problem with bullying.

"I have never spent any time in respite – my family always kept an eye on me. One time someone was calling things at me in the street, but I ignored them and it never bothered me.

"I went on holidays with Destined, and I went to Westport with my sister for a week in August. I don't go with my parents; they are getting too old for that now. I have been single all my life and I am happy with that."

Deirdre has been a member of Destined since just after it opened. The group is the central focus of her social life.

"It first started up in a club called Youth First [in the

Bogside]. Then, we got the premises down in Great James Street where the café is now. And then we moved to Princes Street where we are now.

"I would always come in when I am off on holiday. The people are good, and the workers are great as well. I get on with the people easily.

"Before Destined it was hard to go out and do things. I stayed in the house, sitting doing nothing. Then I heard about Destined, and it made a big difference in my life."

WE'RE JUST LIKE A FAMILY

'Anything you need knitted or crocheted just let me know.'
Kathleen McCrea

Kathleen McCrea, who is 43, has been working in Austin's Cafe for 20 years. A former boarder at Foyle View Special Care School, she now lives in Ardavon House, a semi-independent living facility in Derry.

"I really like Ardavon," she smiles. "I've been here since it opened, twenty-three years ago. The carers are very good to us. Every day we get breakfast and dinner together – sometimes chips for a treat.

"There are twelve of us in the house – we're just like a family. We normally go on holidays together, but last year, one or two didn't feel up to it, so we voted to cancel the trip. We didn't want to split up the group, and we opted for days out instead.

"The helpers at Ardavon [key workers] are great; Anne-Marie, Christine and Paddy. We have meetings to discuss things like the menu and food, safety training and any concerts or nights out we'd like to organise."

Ardavon is one of several semi-independent homes for people with learning disabilities in the Derry area; there are others at Belmont, Trench Road and Hazelbank. The facilities operate with a high degree of transparency; each client retains a charter of their rights on the back of their apartment door. There are also regular snap inspections.

Kathleen was one of the first boarders at Foyle View in the late 1960s and immediately became very attached to her first teacher, the late Isabelle Glenn, who was then appointed her guardian. Foyle View is a controlled, special school for children with severe learning difficulties. It was initially administered by the Department of Health but following changes in legislation in the late 1960s, it is now run by the Department of Education. Mrs Glenn retired as vice-principal of the school in 1994.

The Glenn family continue to act as Kathleen's guardians four decades on – and she still attends all the family functions. She also travels extensively with them. But she has a phobia of escalators, which made a recent trip to London quite challenging...

"I can't get on them," she explains. "And in London they're everywhere. So it meant we had to travel about by bus and sometimes by taxi, as we couldn't use the underground.

"I don't mind lifts so much. In fact, I once helped a woman who started to panic when we got stuck in a lift. But escalators I don't like at all."

Kathleen's experience of the education system was very positive. "I loved Foyle View. It was great craic. I learnt to read, learnt to count and we would sit in circles to listen to stories – or even watch TV sometimes."

She was also entrusted with the daily task of collecting the Glenns' young sons from the Model School and bringing them over to Foyle View, which was then based nearby on Northland Road.

While at the school, Kathleen developed a love for needlework and crocheting – and she spends many hours of her spare time making birthday presents and christening garb.

"I just love going into wool shops," she smiles. "Anything you need knitted or crocheted just let me know."

Her involvement in Destined has really broadened her social horizons. And it has also helped her educational development.

"I've learned a lot about money management from Catherine and Colm. And we sometimes use computers, which I enjoy a lot.

"I've been on holidays with the group; it was great fun. We do the rambling on a Sunday – and I really like it when Rónán brings the dog. And Dympna and I go to the pictures on Friday nights sometimes with the leaders and other times by ourselves."

"I have been involved in doing fundraising for Dr McGinley and the Foyle Hospice for the last twenty-six years. This has included taking part on all the walks and also attending the formal dinners. I intend to continue raising money for the Hospice, as it is a worthy cause."

[See also: George Glenn on page 69]

EXCUSE ME, I AM HERE

'I would have liked to get a wage working in the factory. I only got £15 a week travel allowance and nothing else, which wasn't even enough for the taxi every day. I look after my own money. I have no problems with it.'
Patrick Lavery

Lifelong football fan Patrick Lavery was born in Dundonald Hospital in 1966. He was cared for by the Good Shepherd nuns in Belfast, and later at Termonbacca in Derry, before, aged three-and-a-half, he was adopted by his parents, Mary and Joseph.

Patrick had a happy upbringing in Creggan and got on well with his younger sisters, Joanne and Marie. However, because of his chest condition (he has asthma and a weak heart) he wasn't able for the rough and tumble of street games. "I was excluded, but what can you do if you can't take part? I would play pool though."

Patrick's learning disability became apparent at primary school. He briefly attended two mainstream schools in Creggan, before finally going to Belmont House Special School, which he loved.

"The primary school said I was disruptive to the class, keeping everyone back. I had problems understanding stuff in school. I didn't worry about it though – and still don't. Now I accept what's going on.

"Belmont was a big step to me. I didn't know what was happening or why. They told me I would be best in Belmont, and my parents agreed. I was very happy in Belmont. I must say I never had any problems there. I did the same work as the normal weans do and did it well and had lots of friends. The teachers were very good to me; no one was bad to me.

"I would like to have studied more maths. I was good at maths. I never did any accounts. I didn't do much computers; they only started to come in when I left school in 1982."

Patrick is particularly appreciative of the help he got from Belmont teacher Elizabeth Duddy, who along with his parents was one of the biggest influences on his young life.

Outside school, however, Patrick did suffer from bullying.

"I had problems with name-calling from strangers. I couldn't cope with it. I always went running to my father. He would go out and tell them, 'Don't be calling him names.' I was upset with it. It went on till my teens. I never fought back; I'm not a fighting person.

"My father loved me, and my sisters were good too. I don't get called names anymore."

Aged 16, Patrick started work at the Maybrook Training Centre on the Racecourse Road. He had a talent for woodwork and made bird tables, which were then sold by the centre. He had voluntary work placements at Doherty's Bakery and Diamond's Factory before landing a job at the City Factory, where he worked in maintenance for 15 years.

"I liked it there. It was good craic, and the girls were good to me. The fellas were the usual; they give people stick. But you learn to take it. It wasn't stick about being disabled just stick about the football and stuff when Derry got beat.

"The managers were good too. But I only got £15-a-week travel allowance and nothing else, which wasn't even enough for the taxi every day. I look after my own money. I have no problems with it. I would have liked to get a wage working in the factory."

Ideally, Patrick would have loved to go into catering, and since leaving school he has completed cookery and hospitality courses. And he thoroughly enjoyed the recent spell he spent working in the Irish Café on Great James Street. "It was good, and I got a full salary. I worked there for a year. I speak broken Irish, though. I'm not fluent."

Patrick has a very busy social life, which includes his membership of Destined, nights out at the Don Bar, frequent trips abroad and, of course, his love of football. He is a member the Northside Derry City Supporters Club and has travelled to matches all around the country. "I have been to places like Cork, Waterford and Limerick. It's good craic. There's a lot of singing. They are good chanters. I like the old songs."

In 1994, Patrick flew out to New York for the World Cup and was seated behind the Italian net in the Giants Stadium when Ray Houghton scored the goal that won the game for Ireland.

"Nobody knew it was a goal. Everyone was sitting, then everyone on the far side of the stadium got up because they saw the ball go into the net. Then eventually it travelled round that Ireland had scored." Patrick had travelled to the States with his father and his four uncles. They had saved five pounds a week for the four years running up to the finals.

"Some of us stayed with my uncle over there, he's dead now, and some stayed with an Irish friend of his. We were in Jackson Heights, where the Colombians all are. On July 4, my daddy said he was going out to watch the fireworks. We heard the bangs – but it was real bullets they were shooting in the air. I shouted to him, 'Get in!'"

Despite his health problems, Patrick participates in many of Destined's activities and has several good friends in the group.

"When I go out on the [Sunday] rambling, I have to pace myself. But I still get there. My bad chest slows me down because everybody walks fast. I have asthma, and sometimes it's worse than others. Other than that my disability doesn't slow me down.

"Sometimes I take a drink, up in the Don Bar, maybe two times a week, with people that don't have disabilities. And I would go out with Brian Quigg [Destined member] on Saturdays, though he doesn't drink. I would drink about eight pints a week – four on Wednesday night and four on a Saturday.

"The first time I got out to the Don Bar with my father, they never heard of anyone with a learning disability going for a drink. It was always able-bodied people around bars. I started drinking in it, and they took to me well. I used to be in the syndicate. I would let them do the betting. I would give them a pound a week and they would place the bet."

Patrick is happy to be single and has never wanted a girlfriend, describing himself as too set in his ways. He loves living with his parents and is very grateful for their continued openness with him.

"The public are beginning to realise that people with learning disabilities have to have their say about what goes on in their lives. It's not like the way it used to be, when they were institutionalised and were put away and not allowed to communicate. Groups like Destined have made a big difference

"My parents were very open and told me what was going on. Sometimes other people would talk above me, not to me. But I would interrupt and say, 'Excuse me, I am here.'"

I SAT WATCHING TV, DAY IN AND DAY OUT

> 'Paul, Bridget, Róisín and me founded Destined because there was nothing there for us. I remember the four of us sitting in a wee room alone.'
> **Jim O'Reilly**

Jim O'Reilly, who is 40, is a founder member of Destined and the current committee treasurer. ("I'm the man to see if you need a sub!") A lifelong football fan, he is a regular at the Brandywell, though is a little concerned at Derry's current run-of-form. Jim lives in the Bogside with his mother.

"My mother noticed I had a learning disability as soon as I was born. It has never worried me though; I just get on with my life. We were a happy family."

Jim went to school at Belmont House, where he got on well with his teachers and his studies. He wasn't above the occasional bit of mischief, however, and didn't like getting up in the mornings. "I used to slip in at seven o'clock in the morning to turn my mum's alarm clock off, so I could sleep in. Sometimes it worked too. If it was too late for school, then my mum would just keep me off, and I would just sit around the house doing nothing and watching TV – a perfect day to myself!"

In general though, Jim behaved himself. "I liked going swimming and things like that with the school. I knew most of the teachers. I was never unfairly punished because of my disability or excluded. No-one bothered me."

Outside school, Jim was occasionally subjected to abuse, but his four sisters and two brothers were very protective of him. "Sometimes, when we were going over the street, people would call names at me. I just walked on and ignored it. I had plenty of friends. If anyone was taking the hand out of me, my brothers and sisters would keep me on the straight and narrow – and tell me to walk away.

"Being taunted is very hurtful. I would never respond. Just get on with it, and don't lose your temper. If they keep calling and calling to you, it's best to walk on and keep ignoring them.

"My mother was also very good. My mother and me are very close. If anyone says anything about me, she is very quick to defend me."

Teachers such as Mrs Begley and Mrs Peace were a big influence on Jim. And they helped him develop a keen interest in computers, which he pursues to this day.

"I have taken courses in Destined in IT with Colm and would like to get a job in computers. Dermot sends me emails to check and shows me games to help me learn. If I am on the computer in Destined, there are people there to help me."

Prior to starting up Destined seven years ago, Jim worked as an unpaid gardener in a scheme for adults with learning disabilities. He didn't enjoy the job and hasn't worked full time since. He has plenty to fill his time though, between being a director of Destined and his many social interests.

"In my free time, I go for walks. I used to walk everywhere but I don't like doing it at night now, as it's too dangerous. I can't drive because I am on medication. I do like cars, though.

"I also play pool and Playstation games. I don't play football, but I watch it – particularly Celtic. I used to go to all the Derry matches but not as many now because they are playing badly. I live only five minutes away from the Brandywell in Donegall Place."

Jim is also a big music fan, especially the Black Eyed Peas and Elvis, and he loves to watch the pop channel VH1. He doesn't go to concerts though, as they're too expensive.

"I don't manage my own money because I would spend it all. I'm learning now how to manage money."

Destined has made a huge difference in his life for the better. When Jim was at school, after lessons finished or when term was over, he would never leave the house.

"I would just sit watching TV, day in and day out, not meeting anyone. But now, people with learning disabilities are always out.

"I was one of the founders of Destined. Four of us decided to set up a group, then we got premises, and we started out from there. It changed my life for the better. Paul, Bridget, Róisín and me founded Destined because there was nothing there for us. I remember the four of us sitting in a wee room alone." The group now has more than 40 members.

While the situation for people with learning disabilities has improved, Jim believes that there is still discrimination in wider society.

"Sometimes people with learning disabilities get ignored.

If someone ignores me, I don't talk to them at all. It annoys me a lot when you say hello to someone, and they just walk right past you. I have had that all my life.

"I have more confidence now than twenty years ago. I have lots of friends so it doesn't bother me as much. I think I am lucky to have a good family and lots of friends."

I SMILE ALL THE TIME

'I accept my learning disability. Sometimes people call me names or say things like, "Look at her" or, "Look what she is doing," and I tell them to shut up.'
Lisa Mallett

Lisa Mallett, who is 35, works at Evergreen Nursery in Stradreagh. She loves fashion and music, and is Destined's in-house style queen. Lisa lives with her parents and two sisters in Bracken Park. They are a very close and happy family.

"My mum and dad are good to me. They help me and they take me out on runs in the car like to Lisfannon or the beach. When we go to the beach, we would take a picnic with us with – sandwiches. I had a nice time growing up. I don't fight with my sisters. But they sometimes take my clothes and I take their clothes as well!"

Lisa was sent to Belmont House School aged four but didn't adapt well to it. "I never liked it. I couldn't speak at school because I was quiet when I was younger."

After transferring to Foyle View Special School, however, Lisa was much happier and made lots of new friends. "My friends were Shauna McKevitt, David McCauley and Patrick Cassidy. At school everyone was mostly good to me. But sometimes my teachers were cross at me and sometimes weren't fair. One teacher slapped me on the leg and stood me in the corner because I was bad – I used to hit people I knew. I was bold, but I don't do that anymore. Mrs Glenn, who died, was my teacher too. She was George Glenn's wife and was very nice.

"Sometimes at school I used to get called names. I haven't forgiven them! And once, I got pushed under the water and I couldn't breathe, when we went swimming with the school. That put me off going swimming."

Lisa has never worried about her learning disability and says she gets great support from her family and friends when outsiders occasionally pass comment.

"I accept my learning disability. I get on grand. Sometimes people call me names or say things like, 'Look at her' or, 'Look what she is doing,' and I tell them to shut up. My mum said to me not to take them on. This happened a couple of weeks ago as well."

After leaving school, Lisa went to work at Maybrook Training Centre and then became a volunteer at Greenhaw Care Centre, before moving to Evergreen in Stradreagh.

"I don't like Evergreen much, but I liked where I used to work before, in Greenhaw. I did the hoovering and washing there on Tuesday mornings and cleaned the tables in the canteen with Clare. At Evergreen, I tidy up the dishes and put the knives and forks on the tables. They are good to me. Dorothy calls for me every morning and takes us to work. I get on well with my co-workers.

"I would like a job doing cleaning, polishing and hoovering. I don't do it in the house though. I write down in my work what I did in the house. I am the only one in the house to take my plate over to the dishwasher after I eat!"

Lisa is also taking courses at the North West Institute and is a regular attendee at Destined.

"The teacher does programs with us at the Tech. He gives us a sheet and spells out the numbers we do. I can't count well or use money. I can write a little.

"I like going to Destined. It's good. I have been going since the start. I enjoy all my friends like Darryl, Kathleen McCrea and Dympna. I like the rambling club and the pampering. I don't go to the pictures on a Friday though. I went on holidays to Belleek with Destined. It was good. And we went on a train to Portrush, to Barry's Amusements, and I went on the Big Dipper. I was squealing out of me. My mum said I was mad going on it. I'm not really scared, though.

"There are lots of carers who are very good to me like Anne Sweeney and Fiona Melarkey and the staff at Destined: Dermot, Terry, Catherine and Martina Coyle."

Besides Destined, Lisa has two other great loves in her life, music (especially the Spice Girls) and style.

"I go shopping in Primark, where my sister works. Sometimes it's good value. I go up every Saturday to Foyleside and the Richmond Centre with my parents. Then they take me in for something to eat in the café.

"When I am going out somewhere, I get my hair done in John Paul's Hairdressers on Carlisle Road. Edel always does my hair – I don't let anyone else do it. I normally go every month, every time it grows.

"I like style. If someone is badly dressed I tell them they shouldn't wear that. I would say to my mother and sisters 'I don't like this' and 'I don't like that'. They don't mind.

"I like to spend time going places. I used to do Irish dancing when I was younger. I had an operation on my foot one time. My foot was very sore. I only dance at discos now."

Lisa says she is a lot happier now, and has a lot more friends, than when she was younger.

"It's better now than when I was young. I am happy now. I smile all the time."

[See also: Kathleen Mallett on page 84]

I DIDN'T WANT TO BELIEVE I HAD A DISABILITY

'Most of the trouble I got into was caused by people calling me names like "spastic" or saying, "You go to Belmont because you are stupid." I was very frustrated and angry. Sometimes I wanted to hit out, and sometimes I did.'
Michael Cole

Thirty-five-year-old Michael Cole is a former full-time Sports Development Officer with Destined. He currently lives with his mother in the Hazelbank area of Derry, but he intends to develop the skills to live independently.

"My childhood was good. It was full of good times and relatively happy memories. My parents got divorced when I was about four years old. But I got on well with my mum most of the time.

"The first primary school I went to was Steelstown – I don't remember much about it as I was only five when I left. Unfortunately I was seeking a lot of attention from the teachers, and they thought I'd be better off in Belmont. When I was growing up I didn't really like the idea of going to Belmont because of the reputation it had for being a school for people with disabilities. I just wanted to be like everyone else and go to a mainstream school.

"I know now that I while I might have learned more in a mainstream school, I would have been bullied a lot more. I was even bullied at Belmont. Some of the boys thought I was too soft and pushed me about a bit, and it was hard to get it stopped because the teachers thought I was provoking it. I was hurt, and there were times I wanted to lash out. But I knew as I got older that this sort of behaviour would get me into trouble. If I'd gone to Carnhill or another school, though, it would have been much worse."

While a teenager, Michael boarded for two years at Greystone Hall Special School in Limavady [now Rossmar Special School], which he enjoyed. But he found being away from home for five days a week too much and persuaded his mother to move him back to Belmont.

During his schooldays, there were times that Michael felt excluded and isolated. And as he readily admits, he reacted badly to rejection – and picked on other people in turn.

"I felt that, while my friends were happy to play football with me, when it came to other things I was left out. Like when they were talking about girls, they would say, 'Don't say things like that in front of him.' I was embarrassed about that because at that time I didn't realise I was different from everybody else. Even now I don't think I am too much different. If they were going out on bikes or up to the 'planting', they would make excuses to make sure I didn't know that they were going. If I did find out, they would just run on. Children are very cruel.

"Most of the trouble I got into was caused by people calling me names like 'spastic' or saying, 'You go to Belmont because you are stupid'. I was very frustrated and angry. Sometimes I wanted to hit out, and sometimes I did.

"I realised myself that I was a bit cruel too to other children. I passed it on down. I am ashamed to say that I wasn't any different than the children who were mean to me, as I did the same thing to people less able than me. I wouldn't really bully them, but I would say things that weren't nice. I think that was a result of my own low confidence. As I grew up, I realised it was wrong."

Outside school as well, Michael could be a bit of a tearaway. But he was quick to learn the error of his ways.

"Me and my brother decided to 'wag' school one day, and we ended up going up the town. We decided to get some lunch, but we had no money. So I went into Dunne's Stores and decided to help myself to a bar of chocolate. But just as I was getting on the escalator, the security man grabbed my left arm and said, 'I saw that.' I was lucky to get off with a warning.

"Other times I would have just acted spoiled and fought with a lot of people, physically and verbally. But mostly it was a reaction to other people picking on me because of my disability or provoking me. And I didn't have the sense to ignore them, like I do now."

A very articulate young man, Michael left school without any formal qualifications. But he has done several courses in literacy and numeracy since then, and would now like to pursue a career in administration.

"There were several teachers who were very good to me. Mrs Mallon helped me a lot; she taught me how to read. She was a nice teacher – I liked her. Mrs Bryce was also very kind.

"Since I left school, I have completed English Entry Level III, and I also did some maths, so my maths has improved as well. I am currently about to start the ECDL [European Computer Driving Licence] at the Tech and I have also started a catering course. The ECDL will be a bit of a challenge, but I know I am able enough for it.

"I would like to work in basic administration. Some people might think it is too high because of the exams needed. But I have found out through Dermot that basic administration doesn't necessarily require exams – that's why I think it is realistic."

Since leaving school, Michael has found it difficult to find full-time employment. However, he did work in Destined for a year as a Sports Development Officer, before the funding for the post expired.

"Before that, I worked in Shantallow Training Services, where I experienced a bit of discrimination from the other young people. But I was also in the Youthways training group, which I liked."

Michael has never been in respite care, though he has been admitted to Stradreagh, as a voluntary patient, on a number of occasions because of mental health issues.

"When I was about eighteen or nineteen, I was in Stradreagh a few times. The staff were generally okay; some were better than others. Sometimes I would have to challenge them to get to do things I would normally be allowed to do. I wasn't really happy there but I knew I wasn't well enough, and I needed to be there. I was a voluntary patient, so it wasn't too much bother when I tried to get out.

"The last time I was in was in 2007. I haven't been unwell since then, so I think it's clear I am on the mend."

Michael's involvement in Destined has, he states, been extremely beneficial for his confidence.

"When I was at school, I didn't want to believe I had a disability. But at that age you don't. As the years progressed I accepted it. I realised it was nothing to be ashamed of. Since I came to Destined I have got a lot more confident and a lot more accepting of my disability.

"I haven't been lonely since I joined Destined. But before that I would have been lonely a lot. Destined has made a significant difference to my life. I am getting out a lot more, doing more things and going more places. I have even delivered speeches in the City Hotel and at the Guildhall, which I wrote myself. I would go out with Destined members from time to time to the Don Bar or the café. I don't drink except on very special occasions, but I like to go out for the craic."

Under Destined, Michael has taken part in the Access to Citizenship programme, which aims to empower adults with learning disabilities.

"I live with my mum, but one of my three goals under the programme is to become confident enough to live on my own. I am going to be doing courses to help me, like cooking and so on. I can't cook now but I can do the basics – beans and toast, and eggs. I can do most of the domestic stuff as well; I just need to learn how to use a washing machine.

"I don't have a girlfriend, but it is something I would think about. We are going to be doing relationship training in November. It's going to teach what skills you need to have relationships – how to go out on a Saturday night and talk."

A self-confessed football nut, Michael spends a lot of free time following his beloved Liverpool. He also likes listening to music, reading and watching TV.

He believes that support for people with learning disabilities is improving – but still isn't perfect.

"People understand more. There are still some people out there who will never be educated and probably don't want to be. There's still the odd young person who would shout something. But if you don't respond to them, it's not giving them a laugh. That's the way I see it."

MY FRIENDS DON'T SEE THE DISABILITY, I'M JUST ME

'I think it was unfair how people bullied me. I got very upset and I used to go home crying. It's made me stronger. I just think of all those people and say, "Well look at me now." I am happy now.' Róisín O'Hara

Róisín O'Hara is 28 and lives with her fiancé in Derry. The eldest of four children, she attained NVQ qualifications in business and now works as a clerk for a local accountant. A founding director of Destined, she has Asperger Syndrome and cerebral palsy.

Róisín was born in Dublin and lived in Donegal, before her family moved back to Westland Avenue in Derry when she was a young child. She describes her childhood as very happy – and her family as "really close". She attended Belmont and later Foyle View, which greatly developed her confidence.

"I realised I had difficulty learning when I was about six or seven. I was really shy in school and found it hard to understand stuff. Sometimes I felt like it was too much for me. Some of the teachers were very nice; they helped me get through my maths and English and stuff.

"I used to get upset a lot about things like when I made mistakes. But my mum and dad always supported me through my childhood."

Outside school, though, Róisín was occasionally subjected to bullying and exclusion. She was a quiet child, with few friends outside her class.

"People on the street called me names because of the way I walked and because of the cerebral palsy. I used to get left out of things a lot, and I didn't have many friends. I would be ignored a bit and not included in games. After a while I just didn't go out because I had no one to play with. I sometimes played with ones in the street, but a lot of the time I had nobody. Looking back on it now, it was hard sometimes. I used to spend all my time on my own. But my brother and sisters were always there for me. I am the oldest. Me and my brother were always very close."

Róisín started Belmont House Special School when she was five. She was 13 when she met and made friends with Ciara, who brought her out of her shell. Jane Bryce, who taught Róisin at Belmont, was also a great help.

"I met Ciara in second year. She helped build my confidence and stood up for me if anyone was giving me abuse. I would [still] sometimes get abuse, but I didn't let it bother me as much.

"I would have got on along with most of the class, but there were a few who were just trouble. I would keep clear of them. They would be smoking and fighting and picking on people. Some of them thought they were too smart for the school. Jim [Jim O'Reilly, who conducted this interview with Róisín] was an angel compared to some of the ones I knew.

"Jane Bryce in Belmont helped me a lot with my reading, writing and spelling. There were a few other teachers who helped me a lot, if I had any problems. I could just ask in class for help and not feel nervous."

Róisín also completed a number of courses at the North West Regional College, and studied drama in the Playhouse with Pauline Ross.

"At the Playhouse everyone chatted and included me. We were all like friends, even though we didn't know each other very well. And I loved performing drama.

"I was in a play about two Derry girls heading out for the night. We would look in the newspaper trying to find a nightclub, and at the end of the night we shared a taxi. It was just about a typical Derry night out. It was great because I got on really well with everyone, and no one even knew I had a disability. Everyone was just treated as an equal.

"Before we performed it, we used to play games to get to know each other. There was one were you had to fall back and the other person had to stop you from falling. I enjoyed getting to know people, and it helped my confidence."

As well as acting, Róisín studied dance – and is a particular fan of Salsa. And she also took courses in reflexology and aromatherapy; indeed she is so good that she's "tortured" by people looking for her to do their hands and feet.

After school, Róisín had a placement with the Citizens Advice Bureau, where she loved working with manageress Jackie Gallagher. She also had spells with Marks & Spencer and the Housing Executive, before getting her first job as a clerk with Danny McGowan Accountants five years ago. "He is great. He is so easy-going and down-to-earth." Ideally, Róisín would like to work in computers, though she's very happy where she is.

Outside work, she has plenty to keep her busy. She and her fiancé Gary have recently bought a house and have a wedding to plan. They also have two dogs to contend with and a hectic social life.

"I met Gary when I was twenty-three in Earth [nightclub]. We've been going out for five years and we're getting married in two years time at the Cathedral. He's a mechanic, who works in Perfecseal, and is really sound. We're best friends. We bought a house on Helen Street three years ago together. I'd like to go to America for the honeymoon. We have cousins in L.A. – and I've been there twice.

"I don't know if we'll have children, probably not. He has lots of nieces and nephews. I don't mind being an auntie for a few hours and then leaving them back! And we also have the dogs.

"I was nervous telling Gary about my disability; some people just don't want to know. And it's hard to explain to someone that you have a disability. It's very difficult to find people, when you're different. But Gary is a very nice person and sees me as me. His friends too don't see the disability – I'm just 'Róis'. Some people talk down to you and might be patronising, but Gary and his friends are no bother.

"I went out with boys before Gary. One of them broke it off with a text message: 'It's over.' That was cold."

Like most young people, Róisín and Gary enjoy pubs and clubs, including their local, the Phoenix Bar. They also like going to the pictures, dancing, throwing the odd party in their house and sometimes just "chilling out". Plus of course, there's the nightly dog-walking.

"We have two. Muttley is a collie-sheepdog terrier and

the other, Barney, is an Alsatian basset-hound. I walk them most days. Myself and Gary take them to the beach or down along the river, or sometimes out the Northland Road."

The young couple's interests differ dramatically, however, when it comes to cars and fashion. "He's into cars and I'm not. I can't drive but I want to learn to cycle. Then, when I talk to him about fashion, he looks at me like I have two heads."

Facilities and support for people with learning disabilities have improved over her lifetime, says Róisín. But there's still a long way to go.

"Some things still annoy me, like people talking down to me. I still notice that sometimes they talk like you can't understand stuff. When I was younger some people would ask my mum and dad how's Róisín doing, and I would be sitting there thinking, 'Why don't you talk to me?' I felt like they thought I was my disability and not *me*. I felt invisible sometimes.

"I think it's good nowadays because there are groups like Destined. And it's easier to get work experience to get people to do jobs. It gives you more confidence.

"I found it hard growing up because of my learning disability and people making fun of me. I have got more confident over the years because of certain people in my life. I think it was unfair how people treated me or just bullied me because they didn't know me. I got very upset, and I used to go home crying. One time when I was young, I was bullied and had to go to my mum and dad because they wouldn't leave me alone. It's just made me stronger. I think of all those people and say, 'Well look at me now.' I am happy now."

CHAPTER 2

The Invisible Lives of Carers and Guardians

The people interviewed in the following section have devoted the bulk of their lives to caring for children or adults with learning difficulties. Several are professionals in the field, and all are strong advocates for the rights of their charges.

Once again, the stories are presented chronologically, to best highlight the changes that have taken place over the lifetimes of those interviewed.

WE WEREN'T FAR-SIGHTED ENOUGH

'It seems a shame that millions of pounds are invested in the education of people with learning disabilities, in state-of-the-art schools, but suddenly at nineteen there's nothing for them, and they're at the mercy of the health boards.'
George Glenn

When George Glenn began teaching at the new Foyle View Special Needs School in the early 1960s, he had little idea that 40 years on he would be legal guardian to one of its first pupils.

George's late wife Isabelle, who was deputy-principal at the school, took an immediate shine to a three-year-old boarder, Kathleen McCrea – one of the nursery unit's first two new arrivals. And it wasn't long before the "very beautiful, good wee girl" became part of the extended Glenn family. Indeed, one of Kathleen's prized possessions is a photograph of herself, aged six, at the christening of the Glenn's son in 1972.

"Because of her circumstances, she was a boarder," explains George, "so we would take her home with us at Christmas, Easter, and summer – and then more regularly, about once a month. Before long, she was a fixture at all family events. And today she still attends every christening, wedding, funeral and birthday party.

"At the time Kathleen first arrived, Foyle View was quite innovative. There was no Stradreagh Hospital then, which meant that everyone with a learning disability, who hadn't a family, automatically went into Muckamore Abbey in County Antrim. So the new school allowed children from the west of the Province to come back to their own area."

Foyle View, which initially catered for both day pupils and boarders, was located in the grounds of the City & County Hospital on Derry's Northland Road, before moving to its current home on the Racecourse Road.

"At various times Kathleen had ongoing medical problems requiring hospitalisation," says George. "And occasionally she did need intensive nursing care, although ninety-five percent of the time she was fantastic.

"Changes in the legislation meant that Kathleen was able to stay at Foyle View until she was nineteen. After that, she went to Stradreagh for a short time. She was in a family environment there and had a good programme of care, and she still came out to us at weekends and so on. And then twenty-three years ago, she moved into semi-independent housing scheme."

At the time Kathleen left school, George was particularly interested in the transition of people with learning disabilities into the workplace. But the economy was in poor shape in the mid-80s, and even "servicing" jobs in factories (i.e. low-level labouring), which might previously have been available, were dying out.

George, however, was determined. "I was very fortunate to hear about a Government programme that allowed people like Kathleen take up sheltered employment. Then, there were two choices: day-care workshops, which we weren't happy about for a girl of her ability; and a second programme, which enabled an employer to take Kathleen in and assess her work output against a so-called 'norm'. So, for example, if she were assessed at eighty percent, the Government would pay the final twenty percent of her wage."

The second option was much more suited to Kathleen's needs, and she found a placement in Wellworth's café, where she worked happily for a couple of years.

Twenty years ago, however, she got a full-time job in catering in Austin's department store, managing the restaurant's industrial dishwashers. And she now is able to train casual staff in using the machinery.

"I go there to visit her at least once a week for twenty years and have never once reported a dirty dish," grins George.

"The secret is to change the water often," explains Kathleen.

After Isabelle Glenn died in 2002, George and Kathleen took the decision that he should replace his wife as Kathleen's guardian. "Social services contacted me, and asked me if I were prepared to take on the role. And I did it very happily. It entails twice-yearly case conferences about Kathleen's situation and plans; all her needs are discussed with her social worker, doctors and house co-ordinator.

"The decision to become guardian was complicated slightly by the law regarding vulnerable adults, which insists that any time I take Kathleen away for holidays – or even a day out in the car, I bring my sister or another adult. But my sister and Kathleen are both very co-operative about it.

"I would also call into Austin's to see Kathleen once or twice a week, to make sure she's all right – and chat to her about any problem she might be having. Like currently, her church on Strand Road is closing, and that has been worrying her a little."

George is also quick to pay tribute to the support Kathleen gets from the staff at her home, Ardavon House, an independent living facility for people with learning disabilities. "They're very much a family there – there are twelve in the house, and they're all very close.

"Kathleen is also financially independent and gets weekly pocket money and clothes as she needs them."

After retiring from teaching, George went into community work, overseeing various church-led development schemes and urban regeneration partnerships. He still is very active in helping people with learning disabilities and chairs the Foyle Parents and Friends Association. This group is partners with The Cookie Company, a bakery, and Le Bistro, a café, both of which are staffed by trainees with disabilities.

There has been significant change for the good, in his lifetime, he believes, though not as fast as he'd have liked it.

"The major changes in this sector took place in 1968, when new laws were brought in to replace the 1948 Act, which was basic in the extreme. The earlier Act, for example, would have labelled people with special needs as 'ineducable' and would have referred to people as 'morons', 'idiots' and 'feebleminded'.

"The new Act brought the control of people with learning difficulties under the education boards – and not the health boards as it had been previously. It guaranteed education until the age of nineteen – a very enlightened concept at the time.

"The mistake those of us who had lobbied for the change made was in believing that the over-nineteens would then be properly catered for by the health boards. We weren't far-sighted enough. The problem arose because there was never any statutory provision made within the system to take care of someone once they had left school. And while the health boards had a duty of care, more recently they're finding they haven't got the resources to cope."

The Bamford Review of Mental Health and Learning Disability NI (2007) proposed increasing provisions within hospitals and within the community. But Stormont has yet to release the necessary funding to support the plan.

Social outlets are also scant, which is why Kathleen finds Destined so important. She attends the centre at least twice a week.

"There's a great camaraderie here," says George. "And it has really broadened Kathleen's range of interests.

"Groups like Destined, and Foyle Parents and Friends, have made a great difference. The difficulty is in locating funding and making these projects sustainable.

"But there is a real gap after school. To me it seems a shame that millions of pounds are invested in the education of people with learning disabilities, in state of the art schools, but suddenly at nineteen, there's nothing guaranteed for them – and they're at the mercy of the health boards."

Recently, George has been involved in lobbying at various levels of government to have legislation passed during the next session of the Northern Ireland Assembly to allow each person with a learning disability to have a legal statement of a care-plan, addressing their individual needs. He feels that the new laws should be included in the Programme for Government which is currently being planned.

I'D LOVE HIM TO MEET SOMEONE

'I know I'm very protective of him, possibly over-protective – I'd love to wrap him in a blanket of cotton wool. When he was growing up, I did baby him a lot. I would always take his side against his sisters, even when he was in the wrong.'
Mary Jo McEvoy

Mary Jo McEvoy is mother of Michael, 46, a member of the Destined group. Her son was injured in a traffic accident when he was a toddler and has difficulties with his speech.

"There was no help then," says Mary Jo, without any hint of rancour. "It's just the way it was. People didn't know then what they were dealing with. Now they've a name for it – 'learning disability'. There wasn't then. Years ago, they just put them away. But I wasn't going to let that happen.

"I had a younger daughter who was obviously developing quicker than Michael, toilet-training and so on. But there was an attitude, 'Sure he'll be grand – just give him time.' Even the doctor told me girls are sometimes faster.

"At the start, if I'm to be totally honest, I didn't want to accept it – couldn't, either, for a long time. But as soon as I did accept it, it became easier. And I went out looking for every bit of help I could get.

"My husband was in the American navy, so we were able to get an appointment, through the US embassy, with a Harley Street specialist. He recommended I should get Michael into a special needs school. He'd been in Artillery Street Primary School up to then. But the nuns couldn't cope with him and found him disruptive. He was too anxious – he needed individual attention. [Michael talks rapidly and has a speech impediment. Physically, he is a tall, strong and very young-looking man.] I didn't want him to go to Belmont, initially – maybe it was pride – but I didn't want him singled out."

Michael had been knocked down as a two-year-old in a hit-and-run in America. And to this day, Mary Jo doesn't know what effect this had on his condition.

"I used to blame myself. I was always anxious when I was pregnant with Michael. But the doctor assured me this had nothing to do with it."

Michael duly went to Belmont where teachers such as the late Tom Roulston were a great help. He had some teenage difficulties with girls and heartache, which worried his mother. Then at 18, he left school and spent two years on a training scheme, before going to work as a part-time librarian and also with the Sow & Grow project at Gransha.

Sow & Grow provides horticultural training for 30 people with learning difficulties. The workers grow plants from seeds or cuttings and make hanging baskets for customers and corporate clients. Michael has been working there for 25 years – receiving only a travel allowance.

He used to walk the eight-mile return trip to work every day before he passed his driving test at the first attempt – a source of immense pride for both his parents.

"He took lessons for three years. And Richard Edgar at Sow & Grow was a great help to him with his Theory. The other three who took the test the same time as him failed. The day he passed, we threw our arms round him when he arrived home. He just shrugged us off."

Outside work and school, Mary Jo used to worry that Michael was too reclusive. "He never went out; spent all the time in his room – on the computer or reading. He has a huge library. I tried to get him to mix. But it was difficult. I felt very lonely for him. He never really had a girlfriend, and I don't think that's going to happen for him now. I'd love him to meet someone.

"Since he passed his test, he goes out on runs at the weekend with his two friends – both of whom would have learning disabilities. They'd go to Moville or Malin Head. They love it. At the start, sometimes I had to bribe him to go out, by putting petrol in his car. He used to be a bit moody. But he's changed now."

Mary Jo still manages Michael's finances for him and worries what will happen when she's no longer there for him.

"We've set up a trust fund for him which his sister will administer. And we've spoken to doctors who assure us that they will find facilities ideally suited for his needs. Ideally, I would love for him to have a flat or apartment of his own. Though I'm not sure he could handle it. I fear that he'd be vulnerable on his own.

"On the other hand, I know I'm very protective of him, possibly over-protective – I'd love to wrap him in a blanket of cotton wool. When he was growing up, I did baby him a lot. I would always take his side against his sisters [he has four], even when he was in the wrong. And he got a lot more attention – a lot more of my time. I think back then his sisters might have thought I was a bit unfair on them, but they're a lot more understanding now."

Groups like Destined are a great social outlet, insists Mary Jo. "There was nothing for them before that. There's lots of activities – gets him out of that room and away from the computer."

THE SOUTHERN CARE SYSTEM WAS 25 YEARS BEHIND

'We are so lucky in the people we met because of Shaun; quiet heroes and heroines who have made great contributions to this earth but never get, or seek, any credit.'
Bernie Gallagher

When Culmore resident Shaun Gallagher was a young child in Donegal, his mother Bernie went to the doctor to discuss the fact that his learning disability was becoming more and more pronounced. Shaun had been slow learning to walk and was now beginning to take severe seizures.

"The doctor told me, quite bluntly, to put Shaun in an institution and have another baby," Bernie recalls.

"Back in the seventies, there was virtually no educational system in the South for children like Shaun – just institutional care. There was a boarding school, Craig House, in Sligo, but the children could only come home once a fortnight, and the bond was being broken with the parents, who didn't know how to deal with them when they came back."

Bernie, a psychiatric nurse, was appalled – but was also aware that the care system in Northern Ireland for people with learning disabilities was much more advanced.

"The North was at least 25 years ahead," she comments. "The Southern system, to be frank, was useless. There was no psychiatric nurse in the entire Donegal or northwest area for people with special needs.

"There were no day schools which could cater for Shaun in the South, either. So, we had a number of meetings with the staff of Foyle View School and eventually arranged for Shaun to be enrolled as a pupil."

Bernie felt it was imperative that Shaun attend a day school and not a boarding school.

"I used to work with young adults who had been at Craig House. But when they returned home, their parents weren't familiar with their needs and couldn't cope. So, as soon as they were finished school, these youngsters ended up on psychiatric wards. There was nothing else for them. Though at least they had a safe roof over their heads, even if no-one was qualified to deal with them.

"I remember before I ever had Shaun suggesting at a union meeting that we needed nurses for young people with special needs. But there was a fear that we would lose traditional psychiatric posts."

Shaun had previously been at pre-school, where his family could see some progression of improvements; they gauged that he was, perhaps, six weeks behind the others.

After that, he went to Belmont for a brief time, but failed to engage with the school and people.

"But," says Bernie, "as soon as he went to Foyle View, thanks to the fantastic work of Charlie Herron and [the late] Mrs Glenn, he started copying other students and became more involved."

The curriculum at Foyle View was geared largely towards social skills, but after some prodding from the Gallaghers, Shaun received instruction in the "Three Rs".

"I remember our pride when they taught Shaun how to write his name. He would be able to sign for his own passport."

Shaun was Bernie's first child, and it would be another five years before she had her second. "This gave us time to understand Shaun's disability and become familiar with his needs. But a lot of our parenting was trial and error. We did make mistakes – and you can't really afford to make a mistake at all. For example, when we were teaching him to cross the road, I said 'Look up and down' instead of 'Look right and left'. He took me literally, and we couldn't correct him. And it wasn't until he got to Destined that he learned to do it properly."

After leaving school, Shaun worked for Acorn, where he was awarded a City & Guilds certificate in gardening – another source of great pride for his parents. He then worked for the Churches Trust for nine years where he was the only person in his department with special needs.

"He was blessed with a wonderful foreman, Alec Cook, who really protected Shaun. There was one incident at a site when a fellow worker was winding Shaun up but Alec ensured that this was dealt with."

Shaun was later diagnosed with a bi-polar disorder and spent six weeks in Stradreagh Hospital, where Bernie says he received excellent care. "The diagnosis, and medication he was prescribed, made a huge difference in his life."

After leaving the Churches Trust, Shaun took his passion

for landscaping to his family home, where he tends the garden and lawns. And seven years ago, he joined Destined, which, his mother believes, has led to a huge change for good in his life.

"Destined has opened so many doors for him. There's so much to do – rambling, gym, life skills, cooking classes, going to the pictures and drama. And he's now learning how to handle money with Catherine [a Destined leader]. All the leaders, Dermot, Terry, Catherine and Martina are brilliant.

"There's a real emphasis here on becoming independent. And every member of the group is accepted for what they are – without labels.

"Our real hope for Shaun is that he would become capable of semi-independent living. And Destined is helping him achieve that. In seven years, we've seen a huge change in him. Before he joined the group, we couldn't have gone the length of ourselves without taking him with us. Now he's happy to stay in the house on his own."

The friendships Shaun has formed have been key to his enjoyment of the group. "There's marvellous integration. They all look out for one another. Shaun has many friends here – he really loves Bernadette Bradley and Jim O'Reilly.

"Shaun was always bad with change. But Destined taught him how to adapt. Other groups might do great work, but they're often quite regulated and regimented. Destined has rules but there's also a freedom here, which lets every member progress as they are able, without ticking boxes."

Bernie and her family wouldn't change the way Shaun is for anything. She believes they have learned so much from him – and that growing up with Shaun has led to her other children becoming very caring and compassionate.

"Our children benefited greatly from what we learned from Shaun – our tolerance, patience and acceptance of each day being a great day to be thankful for.

"We are so lucky in the people we met because of Shaun; quiet heroes and heroines who have made great contributions to this earth but never get, or seek, any credit.

"I remember someone asking another of my children, who was then about 16, if he'd prefer it if Shaun hadn't had a disability. My son thought about it for a few minutes, then said, 'I don't know – it would be a different Shaun.' I was very proud of him for that."

I TRY NOT TO THINK WHAT WILL HAPPEN AFTER WE GO

'When myself and my husband went on holidays together last year, on our own, we suggested respite to my other daughters. But they went ballistic – and insisted that she stay with them. They wouldn't hear of it.'
Kathleen Mallett

Kathleen Mallett's eldest child Lisa, 35, was diagnosed with a learning disability when she started school. Lisa, who has a learning age of about four-and-a-half, is one of the founder members of Destined.

"We first became aware of a problem after we put Lisa down for Slievemore Primary School when she was four. But I was told instead that she'd have to go to Belmont.

"I was very shocked. I remember lifting her from the meeting and running home crying. I'd never realised there was a problem. The doctors found it hard to credit that I didn't realise there was a difficulty – Lisa hadn't walked until she was three. But I'd never seen anything wrong; she always seemed happy playing with other youngsters."

Kathleen was later advised that the circumstances of Lisa's birth might have been a factor in her disability. Kathleen was in labour for three days, and Lisa's delivery was induced using the vacuum technique.

"A lawyer advised me that I had a case, but I was never interested in looking back."

Lisa went to Belmont, where she refused for years to speak or paint, and was registered as "an elect mute" – despite the fact she never stopped talking as soon as she came home.

"I was going to tape Lisa, just to show the teacher. But instead I arranged for the teacher to call in unannounced to the house after school to see for herself. She heard Lisa talking away and couldn't believe it.

"Lisa just sat in the corner at school. And because of this, she would occasionally get bullied. But when she went to Foyle View, she loved it and started to talk. She became more involved."

There was also an incident involving a boy at school, which both frightened and angered Kathleen. "Some people tried to suggest Lisa was partly at fault. But she's obviously very vulnerable, and I don't think she was properly treated."

After school, Lisa went to Maybrook Training Centre and then Greenhaw. She's currently a member of the Evergreen project in Stradreagh, but Kathleen – and several other carers – are quite unhappy about the facilities there. "They [i.e. the health authorities] say they've no money and have closed some of the better options."

Lisa has adapted well to work, though her mother feels she's inclined to be a little lazy. "I told them to push her a little. Challenge her – and not let her sit back."

Destined, however, has made a major difference in her life.

"Lisa was one of the first members of the group, when it used to meet behind the Bogside Inn. And it has helped her enormously. The members all really look out for one another. Lisa would have a low IQ and not be as advanced as some of the others, but they really take care of her – watch her crossing the road, if she's going to the shop and so on.

"It also gets her out socially. She does go shopping with her sisters, and her father would take her on runs. But when she was younger, it was terribly hard. She would have sat in the house all the time. I used to have to take her everywhere – bingo, visiting, even to parties. I never had time to myself.

"There's something for everyone at Destined – IT, snooker, karaoke, quizzes, rambling, the women's group. Lisa loves the art they do there – and even presented some of her work to the group. She goes out to the pictures with friends from the group and heads off on day-trips.

"She's very comfortable with the people in the group – and chats away about her friends and the leaders. She even went on holidays with them last year."

Kathleen is very praising of the neighbours and various health workers who helped her and Lisa at different stages.

"There were some very important people," she recalls. "The neighbours would all have watched out for Lisa, to make sure she wasn't bullied. And my house nurses, Lisa Harrison and Cathy Jackson, were very good to me."

The holiday with Destined was significant in that it was one of the first breaks Kathleen had from her daughter. She refused to put Lisa in respite care, despite being offered the chance "umpteen" times.

"Even when my husband was in hospital, I wouldn't entertain it. As long as I can breathe, she'll be with me.

"When myself and my husband went on holidays together last year, on our own, we suggested respite to my other daughters. But they went ballistic – and insisted that she stay with them. They wouldn't hear of it.

"I try not to think about what will happen after we go."

It is very unlikely that Lisa will ever be able to live independently or even semi-independently. "I think she'll always need full-time care. For example, she has no idea about money. I decided once to send her down to the shop, with money wrapped in a note, for cigarettes. But she came back with nothing. Three days later, I found the note and the money lying beside a path.

"She looks completely healthy and is very fashionable – loves getting her hair done and being pampered. But she couldn't survive on her own. Sometimes I think I might have been over-protective, but then I remember just how vulnerable she is."

Lisa still has sleeping problems and has suffered from depression but resists attempts to medicate her. Ever fashion-conscious, she is happy, however, to take what her family tell her are "slimming tablets".

"The Destined group has really brought Lisa out of herself and given her confidence. It has changed her life for the good. Before Destined, I used to look forward to Lisa going off to school – or me going off to my own work, as I needed the break. But now, she's doing very well and is very happy."

I WONDERED IF I'D DONE SOMETHING WRONG

> 'Being aware of learning disabilities and having them in your family are two completely different things.'
> **Teresa McDonough**

Teresa McDonough has four children, two of whom have learning disabilities. Darryl, 26, who attends Destined, holds down a full time job and is very close to fully-independent living, while Claire, 24, will always need full-time care.

"Claire is pre-reading and pre-writing and is more severely disabled. Darryl is very independent – and I'm very conscious not to wrap him in cotton wool."

Teresa and her ex-husband knew of the risks before they had children; there were pronounced hereditary factors in the wider family. But the genetic syndrome, which directly affects her two children – and which is carried by her two other boys, has only recently been identified.

"It's so new and rare, it could well be called the 'The McDonough Syndrome'," she explains.

"There's a fifty-fifty chance any of my children, or my boys' children will have it.

"My husband and I were aware on one level what could happen – there were a number of uncles with learning disabilities on my husband's side – but not to the extent that it did. Our first child, Declan was so healthy, with perfect blue eyes and dark hair. But with Darryl and Claire, we knew from early on there were difficulties. I was watching out for it. And you can generally tell by what they're not doing.

"The first sign with Darryl was when the nurse did the so-called Hearing Test at six months. As part of this, she drops an object, and the child is expected to follow it with his eyes. But he didn't do it. The visitor, I remember was very diplomatic about it and allowed me to tell her that something was not right. Rather than the other way about."

Teresa recalls being disappointed and sad for her son. But her own mother had been an instructor at the Adult Learning Centre (precursor of Maybrook Training Centre), so Teresa had more experience in the area than most.

"In saying that, being aware of learning disabilities and having them in your family are two completely different things," she admits. "I remember looking around at my neighbours, with their fully healthy children and wondering if I'd done something wrong."

Teresa has nothing but praise, though, for the schooling her children received in Derry.

"Darryl was at Belmont from the ages of four to seventeen – and did very well there. He was taught by many great teachers, including Mickey Dobbins, who is now head at Foyle View. Tommy McCully and Nuala Begley, the new principal of Belmont, were also wonderful.

"His confidence grew enormously. He was always in the school concerts from the age of six. He then took part in the *feiseanna*. And as he got older he would have acted as compere at the school shows. When he was leaving school, he was selected to give speeches as part of the Transition from School to Work project.

"He was bullied once or twice, but the school have a very good policy and stepped in immediately to deal with it."

The McDonoughs found the health care system more difficult to negotiate, however.

"Initially, I found the system very stressful," recalls Teresa. "I have a very good care worker, Michael McLaughlin, who was always very supportive. But at the start, I didn't want him near me – it was like an intrusion. There was a fear in me that, because I was visually impaired, on my own with four young children – two of whom had learning disabilities, they would take the children away. It was very scary. I used to stay up late at night cleaning the house in case somebody would come in to inspect it. I had to prove to the outside world I could cope."

On another occasion, when Claire had to go into hospital for a minor procedure, Teresa was astounded at the lack of provision for children with disabilities. "She was panicking, and the doctors didn't know how to cope. They're not trained for it. So, I ended up having to go into the theatre to hold her down."

Because of Darryl and Claire's differing needs, Teresa availed of the respite care system and found it worked very well.

"It was great when they were younger. I needed it. I was on my own. Claire was physically quite demanding, while there were behavioural issues with Darryl. But it worked so well for them. Darryl still visits the family he stayed with as a social event now.

"I refused to let them go to Stradreagh, however. After

all, it's a hospital. They don't need to go there – there's nothing physically wrong with them."

Darryl was intent on getting a job after school and set about getting valuable work experience in the retail and catering sectors. But Teresa was disappointed that despite one firm telling him he was "excellent", they wouldn't give him a summer job.

Then, however, following a couple of bitter disappointments, he got a placement at the City Hotel – after which he was offered a job as a trainee chef.

"The staff there are great with him, but they know he always gives a hundred percent. He works sixteen to twenty hours a week, and now has his own bank account – and he gets the Disabled Tax Credit. His next target is to learn to drive."

Outside work, Darryl enjoys the various Destined programmes, plays snooker with his brothers, is a core volunteer at a project for senior citizens (COSY), and he gives talks on disability with his mother in primary schools.

"If anything happened to me," says Teresa, "I would like to think Darryl would be able to live independently. Claire would need a full-time carer. I wouldn't want my other sons to have to take responsibility for her – though I'd like them to be near her."

Teresa has been a long-time campaigner on the rights of the disabled and was a stalwart on the parents committee at Belmont for many years. She now works closely with Disability Awareness. She is very concerned at the current cutbacks in provisions and has lobbied at Stormont on the issue.

"The Trust hasn't been able to increase bed provision

for respite care since the mid-1990s, despite the rapidly-growing numbers of adults with learning disabilities," she explains.

"And the Executive has also announced cutbacks in funding, which have led, in certain cases, to condemned buildings being used for day care units. The Trust here is now looking to find premises for a unit, but they're only prepared to spend £7000 a year."

Another major issue for parents of young adults with learning disabilities is the right to work. "Claire should have the right to contribute in some way – in a way that's she capable of. I don't expect her to do something that would be beyond her. I myself have only twenty-five percent vision and so wouldn't apply for a job as a driver. But she should have the right to play a role in society."

Darryl is immensely respected by his peers and, indeed, by his neighbours young and old. As yet, he hasn't had a relationship.

"I'd love for him to meet a nice girl," admits Teresa. "I sense a loneliness in him sometimes. With Claire, it used to break my heart that there would be no boyfriends and no wedding day. But then my other son assured me that if he ever gets married, Claire will be a bridesmaid – and we were all thrilled with that.

"In general, there is an openness now about disability that wasn't there when they were younger. They're not treated like lepers, not hidden away. There's still a certain amount of stigma – but there's a lot less of the 'Does he take sugar' type of attitude.

"In saying that, a lot of people don't like being branded with the 'learning disability' tag either. It still rankles with them."

PEOPLE WITH DISABILITIES ARE STILL EXPLOITED

'I still don't think it's right at those crucial times in family life – school entry level, age eighteen, and when parents are ageing and frightened for the future.'
Paula McNamara
(née Quigg)

Brian Quigg, who's 38, and his sister Paula McNamara, who's six years older, both suffer from congenital eye-problems and attended special schools in Dublin. Both are legally blind, though Brian has a little more eye-power and is a "great guide dog" around the mazy Derry streets, according to Paula.

Brian also has a learning disability and is epileptic. But Paula entered mainstream education, under a groundbreaking new programme in the late 1970s, and sat her Junior Cert and Leaving Cert. She went on to university in England and worked as a computer programmer with the Eastern Health Board in Dublin, before becoming an advocate for people with both intellectual and physical disabilities.

Paula initially attended Nazareth House School in Derry. "My parents were very progressive," she recalls.

"They wanted to educate us in a 'normal' school. But the support structure wasn't there. Because I couldn't see the blackboard, I quickly fell behind the others, so the teachers suggested I should go to Jordanstown.

"It was a bit traumatic, as I was expected to board. And I was a bit disruptive for a while, but it was a great school."

At the height of the Troubles, the family moved south to open a fruit-and-veg business. And Paula transferred to a boarding school for the visually-impaired in Dublin, where she was joined by Brian, who later transferred to a secondary school for boys in Drumcondra.

Both had a very positive experience of the education system. Brian, despite his shyness, took part in the school plays and musicals. And he also enjoyed pottery, arts and crafts.

"People at school were all very good to me," says Brian. "I was never bullied. Sister Kevin, I remember, was very kind. And Mary Leonard was a great help as well. I was very well-behaved at school though." Paula rolls her eyes at this suggesting her path mightn't have been quite so smooth. "He was always the pet," she sniffs.

After school, Paula attended the Royal National College for the Blind in Hereford, grant-aided by the South's National Rehabilitation Board.

"There were very few career options for blind people in Ireland at the time," she explains. "You had telephony, social work, physiotherapy, music and maybe one or two other paths. But I wanted to try my hand at computers.

"The college experience was a bit mad for all of us, given that everyone had spent the past fifteen years in a very sheltered environment. There was a lot of partying!"

After working in computing, Paula subsequently qualified in Rehabilitation, supporting people with intellectual and physical disabilities to achieve their goals in training or independent living. She worked first as a case manager with the Health Board and is now a Human Rights Officer with the St John of God healthcare organisation, all the while remaining an activist in the fields of human rights and disability.

Paula's skill in rehabilitation has proved invaluable in assisting her brother in the North. Brian currently lives at home with his parents, who are in their seventies. But he is participating in the Access to Citizenship programme, which aims to empower adults with disabilities, and hopes to get his own place within the next couple of years.

"The main problem getting a suitable place is that the system is so scattered," explains Paula. "There are some places that would be ideal for him, but he has to negotiate three different waiting lists through three different agencies. It's mad."

Brian has completed money-management courses and is able to handle his own budget. He can also read, assisted by a magnifying glass, and can dose out his own medication.

He is largely very positive about the idea of independent living. "I would prefer to have somebody nearby in case I had a problem – within the same house. But I wouldn't have any bother with the likes of tablets or anything like that."

Brian is also very appreciative of Paula's help, laughing that he doesn't mind when she bosses him about the odd time. "I love the banter," he says.

Paula would love to see Brian in a salaried job and is unhappy at the "tokenistic" payments he has received from previous employers.

He currently works at a health centre on a voluntary basis, doing a job his sister believes should be salaried. He spent four years after school in Maybrook Training Centre – "wasn't too bad, but it could be boring" – and he had a work placement at a power station. He has also been a charity collector, scratch-card salesman, and worked at a local supermarket, where, again, he wasn't paid.

Paula often feels obliged to speak up on behalf of her brother, who is good-natured to a fault and never complains. On the one occasion Brian was bullied at work – a co-worker at the power station punched him in the stomach – somebody else had to register the complaint with the Foyle Trust.

"The guy told me 'don't touch the radio unless it belongs to you'," says Brian, attempting to rationalise the attack.

Paula was angry when she heard. "No-one in the family knew about it, Brian hadn't told them," she recalls. "The offender was spoken to, though he wasn't sacked. I think it would have been very different if Brian hadn't had a learning disability."

Paula enjoyed an active social life through college before marrying Paul, whom she had first met many years previously when he attended a dance at her all-girls secondary school as an "approved" escort.

"The nuns would bring in vetted boys to dance with us, but Paul got in by accident," she quips. "I then met him years later at a housewarming party and we hit it off."

It didn't take Paul long to prove himself to Paula's

parents. On the first night he arrived to meet them, he was taken with the rest of the family to the back shed, where he got to spend the next three hours bagging potatoes for grocery sales.

Paula had to overcome some concerns her future in-laws had about her disability. It wasn't an easy process, but she got there. She and Paul are foster parents.

Brian's social life, meanwhile, developed significantly after he joined Destined. "It really took him out of himself," says Paula. "It's been huge. Prior to Destined, his social life consisted largely of his family and his music."

Brian agrees. "Destined gets me out a lot. I go to the centre three or four times a week – more even. I have the Irish class on a Monday, and would usually call in on a Tuesday and Wednesday – and we would sometimes go to the pictures on Friday night with Dermot or Caroline. Then there's meetings here on Thursday. I've also done the Access to Citizenship programme recently, which was very interesting. And we'd go to Derry City matches now and again with Terry McDevitt [Destined leader]."

Brian has taken part in several courses through Destined, his favourite being reflexology with Alexis. "It really helps you to relax," he comments. "It's very calming." He also unwinds by listening to Irish music – everything from Paddy Reilly to the Pogues. And he has got a ticket to the Horslips reunion concert.

As yet he has no girlfriend or partner. "I'm happy to be single," he says, "but I wouldn't rule out meeting a girl in the future."

Paula believes the situation for people with learning disabilities has improved significantly since she and Brian were children, but she's concerned that there are still major gaps in the system.

"It's so much better now," she says, "but I still don't think it's right at those crucial times in family life: school entry level, age eighteen, and when parents are ageing and frightened for the future.

"The positives are that we're no longer putting people in institutions. There are other options. People go through the mainstream school system. Education is so much better. For example, if you've a disability you're entitled to support to get third-level education in the South.

"Things start to fall apart after school or college. Many people with disabilities can't get a job – Brian has been exploited regularly, never receiving a proper salary, despite his skills. The services aren't joined up and are underfunded. Fantastic case workers are overstretched, and because of this, young people are left stuck at home.

"In the Republic, Programmes for Lifelong Learning, which would help people with significant disabilities after eighteen, stalled because of cutbacks. And there are blockages throughout the entire system – people can't be released from acute hospitals because there's no space for them in a rehab hospital, and people can't be released from rehab hospitals as the HSE can't fund their care packages in the community."

APPENDIX

Interview Questionnaire

The reporters agreed this questionnaire as a starting point for the interview process. Questions were chopped, changed, amplified and reworked to suit.

1. Tell us about your childhood. How did you get on with your parents and brothers and sisters? Were you a happy family? Where did you live? What games did you like to play?

2. When did you first realise you had difficulty learning? Did you worry about or accept it? Do you worry about it now or accept it?

3. How did you get on at your first school/primary school? What problems did you encounter there because of your learning difficulty?

4. Were you treated differently because of your learning difficulty? Was there anybody that was especially good, or unpleasant, to you?

5. Do you think you were ever unfairly punished because of your learning difficulty? Can you think of any particular examples of this – any stories you remember?

6. Have you ever spent time in foster care? Did it help you? Was there anybody that was especially good, or unpleasant, to you?

7. Have you ever spent time in an institution for people with learning difficulties? If so, which one? Did you agree to being there? Were you happy there? Was there anybody that was especially good, or unpleasant, to you?

8. Which school or institution that you attended did you most <u>enjoy</u>? Why? What did you enjoy about it?

9. Which school or institution that you attended did you most <u>dislike</u>? Why? What did you dislike about it?

10. Who are the teachers or carers that have helped you most in your life? How did they help you – what did they do for you?

11. What courses did you study? How did they help you develop? Did they help you find a job?

12. What jobs have you done? How did you get on with your co-workers?

13. What job would you like to do?

14. How do you like to spend your free time? Who do you like to spend time with and why?

15. Have you a husband, wife or partner? If not, are you happy with the single life?

16. Would you say the support for people with learning difficulties is better now than it was when you were younger? What has got better? Has anything got worse?